I0411043

Jealousy: Self-Help Guide To Overcome Jealousy Self-Esteem, Insecurity, Trust and Communication In Relationships

5 Practical Exercises to Cope With Jealousy

By Katey Lyon

ISBN-13: 978-1537573403
ISBN-10: 1537573403

entertainment purposes only. Every attempt has been made to provide accurate, up to date and complete, reliable information. No warranties of any kind are expressed or implied. Readers acknowledge that the author is not engaging in the rendering of legal, financial, medical or professional advice. The content of this book has been derived from various sources. Please consult a licensed professional before attempting any techniques outlined in this book.

By reading this document, the reader agrees that under no circumstances is the author responsible for any losses, direct or indirect, which are incurred as a result of the use of information contained within this document, including, but not limited to, —errors, omissions, or inaccuracies.

Katey Lyon

Table of Content

Katey Lyon

"A competent and self-confidence person is incapable of jealousy in anything. Jealousy is invariably a symptom of neurotic insecurity."

Robert A. Heinlein.

Katey Lyon

Introduction

"Jealousy is nothing more than fear of abandonment."

What is jealousy and how to cope with it is something you should learn if you want to build and maintain a healthier relationship with your friends, family, and partner. Although it's okay to be jealous sometimes, it is not right for you to allow yourself to be consumed by such a distressing negative emotion.

Keep in mind if you do not work hard in controlling your jealousy, then your relationship with other people will be at risk of being totally damaged.

In your attempt to learn more about what jealousy is and what usually triggers it, you have to find out more about its most basic categories.

One category is the healthy form of jealousy. This type is not considered to be harmful and can be defined as common envious reactions often faced by couples. The best thing about this kind of jealousy is that it is not difficult to deal with because it is only mild and happens occasionally. Youalso do not need to undergo a lot of mind training when it comes to coping with it.

The other category is referred to as the destructive kind of jealousy, and this is something you should avoid. This type can make you feel jealous in an intense, irrational and frequent manner. If you want to live life with utmost satisfaction, then you have to look for ways to avoid this uncontrollable emotion.

The purpose of this book is to help you to understand jealousy and give you some advice and exercises on how to overcome it.

Sincerely,

Katey Lyon

"Jealousy is simply and clearly the fear that you do not have value. If you can't love yourself, you will not believe that you are loved".
Jennifer James.

Katey Lyon

What Is Jealousy

Jealousy is when you feel unhappy or angry because you believe someone you love (such as your husband, wife, girlfriend, boyfriend) likes or is liked by someone else. Jealousy is an unpleasant emotion you feel when you think someone's trying to take what's yours.

When you experience jealousy you are likely to feel negative emotions such as:

- Inadequacy
- Frustration
- Resentment
- Anger
- Hurt
- Suspicion

Therefore, jealousy is an emotion that contains fear, humiliation, and anger. Jealousy is a comparison, a feeling of being replaced and having some sort of competition.

Some jealousy is normal, but you have to know when you are crossing the line:

- Always demanding attention
- Obsession about where he/she is and with whom
- Accusing of flirting
- Reading his/her messages online/mobile
- Smelling her/his clothes
- Searching their pockets
- Making him/her wrong for wanting to see his/her family and friends
- And much more.....

Difference between jealousy and envy

The first difference to keep in mind is that envy involves two people. One person is envious of another. With jealousy more than two people are involved and involve preserving special friendships due to the involvement of others. It is possible to experience jealousy and envy at the same time. For example, you might be jealous of the attention your boyfriend is receiving from a woman you envy for her physical qualities.

The philosopher John Rawls distinguishes between jealousy and envy because jealousy implies the desire to keep what one has and the envy of the desire to obtain what one does not have. People who are envious can experience painful and overwhelming emotions because someone else has something they don't have. For example: She can buy more things than me because she has more money.

Another example is he / she has more money, a new kitchen or a car that I cannot have. Envy is a symptom of desire that is rooted in a depth or internal emptiness and low self-esteem.

Jealousy is not seen as a primary driving force. It is more of a common experience that we could all relate to.

People who are jealous may also experience negative thoughts, feelings, and anxiety, possibly obsessively thinking about events that may or may not be occurring. They will put themselves in negative situations that reinforce their beliefs. Many confront others, while others hide and separate from people and situations.

Jealousy is more a symptom of insecurity and lack of confidence in the ability to maintain strong and healthy relationships with others and success in other areas of life. Very often jealousy and love are closely related, but in the words of Havelock Ellis: "Jealousy, that dragon that kills love under the pretext of keeping it alive. "

Jealousy is characterized by anger, fear, resentment and insecurity. They are an adjective and people are jealous when they are afraid of losing something they already have. On the other hand, envy is characterized by feeling resentment and longing for something that we do not have. It is a verb and people are envious of something they don't have.

Types of Jealousy

There are many types of jealousy, and all kinds of people often experience these at some point in their lives. Jealousy happens when one is worried, angry and anxious. It is an emotion that makes people dwell on negative things that add more to the anxiety he or she feels.

Jealous people tend to be subjective and view things personally. It is, therefore, necessary to know the different types of jealousy so people will be aware of their emotions and can learn to handle such feelings. In families, jealousy can happen, especially in brothers and sisters. It can also occur among relatives such as cousins. This type of jealousy crops up when more attention is given to a particular family member than to another.

Jealousy can also transpire among friends. In school, jealousy can erupt in school activities when one person is favored more than his or her friend. It is a competition that can turn sour if not handled well. Ideally, competition should be clean and friendly so people will work for their betterment without hurting anybody else along the way.

In couples, romantic jealousy almost always happens. This is when a person feels suspicious about his or her partner's friendship or communication with other people, especially those of the opposite sex. This kind of suspicion usually signifies one's insecurity. If a person is secure in his or her partner's love, jealousy will never happen.

Another type of jealousy is power jealousy, which usually happens in the workplace among personnel. If a certain worker is given a promotion, there are others who may feel jealous about this. When this type of jealousy happens, rumors spread so as to ruin that person's reputation.

Jealousy is normal among people. It usually occurs when somebody else gets the desires of another person. This type of jealousy can be handled without difficulty, but if not given attention, it can make a person self-destruct, as his or her wishes become someone else's reality. Jealousy becomes abnormal when a certain person can no longer hide his or her insecurities, anxiety and worry. This type of jealousy can do one harm or cause harm to somebody else.

Fear of rejection is a cause of jealousy. When a person in a relationship notices his or her partner is talking to someone else, he or she may interpret it in a negative way. One may think his or her partner is already interested in someone new;thus, he or she is scared the partner may leave them.

Another cause of jealousy is insecurity. Because one does not feel good about him or herself, everybody becomes a threat or a potential enemy.

To handle jealousy, it is vital to accept that one is jealous and to assess the reason behind that feeling. It is important for one to stop for a while and analyze why he or she is jealous. If one learns to accept this emotion, it willbe easy to handle it. When acceptance comes in, the resolution will soon follow.

When one is aware of the different types of jealousy, theycan identify his feelings, accept them and do something to counteract them.

Mayor Causes of Jealousy

"Jealousy is that pain which a man feels from the apprehension that he is not equally beloved by the person whom the entirely loves."

Joseph Addison.

If you are currently in a romantic relationship, then the feeling of jealousy is sometimes unavoidable. This holds true if you and your partner have been together for quite some time now and your relationship is already gearing towards a serious path.

If your jealousy is only mild and it does not occur in a more frequent manner, then rest assured that it is just normal, and it is not alarming. But if you already have the tendency to get irrational because of your jealousy and your whole life and your relationship with your partner is already affected in a negative manner, then you are advised to do something to get rid of this negative emotion.

The most efficient way to deal with jealousy is to learn the causes of jealousy so you can act on it in the most appropriate manner possible. The usual causes include the following:

1) Having an untrustworthy partner. If you have a romantic relationship with someone who has cheated on you in the past or who has the tendency to flirt with others, then your jealousy has a legitimate reason. However, you have to understand that jealousy is still a negative emotion, and no matter how good your reason is in feeling this way, you cannot still expect it to serve a useful purpose. Do not allow jealousy to rule your mind and your relationship if you want it to work out.

2) Insecurity. This arises if you have any doubt in your current love relationship. If you are insecure, then there is a great possibility jealousy will get in the way of your relationship. To deal with this, you have to start building your

personality and your confidence. Make sure you do not belittle yourself and start believing you are unique from the others.

3) The need to control your partner[2]. This is also another of the major causes of jealousy that is quite difficult to control. This happens when your partner goes out with his or her friends, and you feel extremely jealous because you are unable to controltheir activities. If you feel the need to control is the cause of your jealousy, then you have to make a self-reflection. You have to start figuring out why you often feel the need to control others.

If you are extremely desperate to control your partner's every move, then it is advisable for you to seek counseling, as this will help you with your problem.

4) Fear[3]. This can trigger you to feel jealous. If someone cheated you in the

past, then it is possible you will also feel like your current partner will cheat on you.

You will be afraid that your partner will meet someone who is better than you and leave you because of it. No matter how strong your feeling of fear is, you have to do something to avoid it from causing you to feel jealous.

Ways To Deal With Some Causes Of Jealousy

Mentioned above are among the major causes of jealousy, and you have to find out which among these causes is most applicable to you. Once you determine what triggers you to feel such a distressing emotion, then you will be on your way towards finding the most suitable solution for it.

1. Deal with your feelings of insecurity. You have to start dealing with your insecurity issues. You have to work on

your self-image and start loving yourself more.

2. Dealing with your fears. Whatever the kind of fear you are experiencing, dealing with your fear will help you to overcome jealousy. Fear of abandonment is the most important one. You can also work on fear of rejection.

3. Try to control your anger. If you are feeling jealousy, you must feel anger. Feeling anger will destroy your relationships. Start now with an anger management course.

4. Assertiveness will help you to overcome jealousy. Being assertive will help you to communicate your needs without being aggressive and without violating other people's rights. Being assertive will help you to stand up for your rights and needs. You will be able to speak up for yourself.

Tips for Coping with Jealousy

There are many ways to cope with jealousy. Jealousy is a natural human emotion and occurs in any relationship. It happens to families, couples, and friends. It is important to deal with it in a rational way because if you act irrationally about it, it may destroy you and your relationships. Follow the tips to handle fits of jealousy in this article.

•If you are with your partner and he talks to another girl, you should just relax and do something else to distract yourself. This will prevent you from doing or saying something you will regret later on. You can talk to someone or look for something you can do as you wait for the conversation of your partner to end. This will distract you and make you put any feelings of jealousy or resentment aside.

•It would also be better if you talk rationally with your partner about anything that made you jealous. Make sure you discuss it with them alone in your house where no one can hear you. Be calm and explain how you feel. Ask him or her to be sensitive to your feelings and to never allow such a thing to happen again.

•People who usually feel jealous have very low self-esteem. It shows they have much insecurity about themselves. If you are one such kind of guy, you must find activities that will make you feel good about yourself. You can learn a new and enjoyable hobby, doregular workouts, do some gardening which is therapeutic or get a makeover.

•Focus on yourself instead of your partner or theperson who makes you feel jealous. Remember to love yourself always. Remind yourself also that you are a beautiful person inside and out. If you always find yourself becoming jealous of even small things, this is not healthy. Get a hold of yourself and forget all suspicions crossing your mind. You may ruin your relationship instead of fixing it. You can overlook a jealous fit by concentrating on other things such as work, an ongoing conversation around you or the ingredients you need to cook for dinner.

•When you feel jealous, avoid alcohol as this make you more irritated, insecure and confrontational. Redirect your feelings to something positive by thinking about good times or things that make you happy. You can also exercise, as working out releases endorphins or the feel-good hormones which help in coping with jealousy.

•If you think your jealousy is already destroying your relationship, better go to a psychologist and get counseling therapy. This will help save your relationship from being wrecked. An expert therapist willbe able to take you to the origin of your problem. He willalso be able to address your insecurities and help you build your confidence.

Jealousy is not abnormal. Just because you feel jealous does not mean you are less of a person. The most important thing is you address issues that make you envious so that things will be normal in your relationship. As long as you are sincere in coping with jealousy, everything will be okay.

5 Practical Exercises To Cope With Jealousy

Exercises 1: What is the root of your Jealousy?

When Jealousy becomes a toxic emotion, you manipulate your loved one in a relationship. You do not believe you are lovable enough and that you don't deserve love. You are afraid to lose this person.

This is the case when low self-esteem plays a role. When you are insecure about yourself, you will exaggerate events.

What is the root of your jealousy?

- Insecurity
- Feeling of Inadequacy
- Low Self-Esteem
- Fear of Abandonment

Insecurity

One of the best ways to overcome insecurity issues in relationships is to stop focusing on how the other person might feel. Usually, this is what we do: Is he/she angry at me? Why did they say that? Why is he not bringing me flowers anymore? And so on. Stop taking things personally. If your partner is angry, do not think that is always because you did something wrong and made him that way. Maybe he/she had a bad day at work, maybe somebody insulted him/her, etc.

Two things you have to start working on:

1) Build your self-confidence: The best way to build your confidence is to believe in yourself. Make a list of your successes. Start making this list from birth. For example, I successfully learned to walk when I was one year old. I successfully learned to ride a bike when I was 8, and so on till your present time. Make a list of 100 things you were successful at through your life. Many times, we take small successes for granted. Now you want to become aware of them. The second

step in building your confidence is to keep your commitments.

Let's say that you agree on working out three times a week. Just do it. When you keep your agreements, you begin to believe in yourself. Is like when you were a child and your mother promised to buyyou ice cream.If she did it, you believed in her, but if she did not you started doubting her. The same goesforthe relationship you have with yourself.

2) Work on your self-image: Self-image is the mental image orconcept one has of oneself. Let go of the idea you are not good enough, are a failure, incompetent and so on. Write down the positive qualities about yourself. Make a list. Start with I am. For example, I am capable, I am artistic, I am caring, I am creative, I am dependable. Write down at least 100 positive qualities. You can also add a small description beside them. For example, I am dependable means that people can rely on me. My boss told me the other day that he trusted me because I was

always dependable and he could count on me to get things done.

Feelings Of Inadequacy

Feeling inadequate means you feel you are not good enough and usually comes as aresult of you believingother people are better than you. Feeling inadequate also means you feel inferior to others.

When you feel inadequate, you might try to hide this feeling by isolation, overeating, overspending, etc. You might also experience low self-worth, fear of rejection, feeling powerless and are not able to accept praise.

What can you do about it?

1) Try to figure out the root of your feelings. You might ask yourself the following questions:

•Have you been put down in the past?
•Are you ignoring your accomplishments?

•If you are a parent, do you struggle because you cannot adequately provide for your children financially, physically or emotionally?

•Do you feel inadequate because other people are more successful, have power or are beautiful and you don't or aren't?

2) If you feel inadequate, it means you feel inferior to somebody. Who is this person? Try to be specific. Do you feel inferior to someonewhois more attractive, hasmore money, is more successful?

3) If you feel inferior, it means you want to be like someone else. Try to stop wanting to be like those people and do not worry about what others think.

4) Focus on your positive qualities. When you feel inadequate, you put your emphasis on what you do not have.

5) If you keep comparing yourself with others, you will end up with a long list of people who are better than you.

Stop comparing yourself with them. You will always find someone who has more than you, or is more attractive, etc.

Low Self-Esteem

Take a piece of paper and write down:

- 10 Strengths
- 10 Favorite things about yourself
- 10 Top achievements in personal, academic, career and relationships

Then write down:

- 10 Ways you can reward yourself
- 10 Things you could do to help somebody
- 10 Things you like doing that make you feel good

Fear Of Abandonment

Fear of abandonment usually comes from childhood loss, like loss of a parent in any form (divorce, death, adoption, etc.). The root of fear of abandonment might also be related to emotional neglect like when parents ridicule children, lack of affection, etc.

If you suffer from fear of abandonment you are likely to struggle with anger, mood swings and low self-esteem.

4 Things you can do to overcome fear of abandonment:

• Build trust in relationships
•Take care of yourself
•Communicate your needs in intimate relationships
•Learn to relax; stress is a cause of anxiety

Katey Lyon

Exercise 2: - Building Self-Esteem

Building self-esteem is a process. However, you can start taking steps and feel good about yourself.

I would suggest that you first find the causes of your low self-esteem. Some causes could be:

• Parental Negligence

• Past Failures

• Child Abuse

• Excessive Criticism

• Bad physical appearance

• Adverse experiences that are not resolved

Choose one of the causes and work on it. For example: Let's say that you identify as one of the reasons is past failures. Concentrate on your accomplishments.

Make a list. Take those failures as learning experiences.

Take a piece of paper and divide it into two columns.

- On top of the left column write the word: Failures,
- On top of the right columns, write the word: What I have learned.

Write down at least ten failures and what you have learned about them.

The second step is to look after yourself. This is a must. You have to start taking care of yourself to feel good about yourself. Just do small steps:

1.Eat healthy
2.Get adequate sleep
3.Workout

After a while of doing thesethree things, you will notice the changes in yourself.

The third steps is to let go of your need to be perfect. No one is perfect, so you shouldn't expect that of yourself or your partner. Perfectionism is a sign of low self-esteem.

Katey Lyon

Exercise 3: Developing communication skills

Effective communication includes the way we talk, how well we listen, and our body language. Most people in relationships, even couples who have been married for many years, can improve the way they communicate with each other in their relationship.

Above all, when there are disagreements or conflicts, it is of vital importance to communicate instead of laying blame. There are several ways to achieve this.

Learn to listen. Listen first, talk later. You will have your chance to say what you feel. Make sure to listen to the other person first. In life, there are always more people wanting to talk than willing to listen. For your relationship to be a joyful one be different than the typical person and learn to listen first.

Do not argue. You can disagree without argument if you recognize the other person's position is to be respected, even if you still can't agree with it. And who knows? You may even learn a new perspective If you just consider what the other person is saying.

Turn your complaints into requests. Never demand as a right what you can always ask for as a favor. Follow this guideline and watch your relationship become better than it has ever been before.

Ask yourself how you might be contributing to the problem. Always assume, first, that you might have done or said something wrong. The other person may be in the wrong, but never assume that first. You have heard that there are two sides to every story. Well, lots of times there are 20! Consider all angles first before you make up your mind that she/he is wrong.

Avoid mind reading. Even those of us who allegedly have psychic abilities aren't mind readers. Never read into things, use your rational mind and ask the right questions to the other person. Never say: I know what you are thinking...

Exercise 4: Developing Self-Acceptance

To develop self-acceptance you have to practice self-kindness. You must stop your habit of self-judgment. Self-judgment causes self-denigration in which you criticize, punish and treat yourself without kindness.

The most powerful way to undo the effects of self-denigration is kindness and forgiveness, which restores awareness of your innate goodness.

To accept yourself you must love yourself, which means you must take time for yourself, ask for help when you need It and have your needs meet.

Exercise:

The best way to start practicing self-kindness is through forgiveness.

Forgiveness is a choice that will help you to feel better about yourself and increase your self-esteem. Forgiveness is a choice to love yourself more. I have become aware that there are a lot of misconceptions about what forgiveness is, and I would like to point out what it is not:

- Forgiveness is not denying what happened. Is not justifying the behavior of the other person. By forgiving, you are not saying that what the person did is ok.

- Is not freeing other people. Is about freeing yourself from the anger, resentment, violence, and revenge. It is an internal process.It isfreeing yourself, not the other person.

- Forgiveness does not mean you have to continue seeing the person whohurt you. Once forgiving is done, you have the choice to move on. You can choose to see the person whohurt you or not. It isa choice.

- To move on does not mean you are holding onto resentment. It is an opportunity to surround yourself with more loving people. To move on is also making a decision to stay or to leave. Some people will say that because you are not seeing that person anymore, you are holding onto resentment, but it is not true. You decide what you want to do and what is better for you.

• Forgiveness is not to avoid somebody. If you truly forgive someone and let's say that you have to keep seeing him/her for some reason, you can do it. It is being open and flexible because you do not hold resentment anymore. Once you forgive you are free of the emotional charge. If you forgive, you won't have any problem talking to that person again.

• Is not merely telling the other people you forgive them; it is an internal process that you do to yourself.

The importance of forgiveness

Why forgiving? Because when you forgive you can move on in your life. Keeping resentment, violence and the desire for revenge will drag all your energy. It will make you frustrated and you will eventually end up with depression.

By willing to forgive you are allowing yourself to stop wasting time and energy on anger. And use that power you regain by forgiving to do something for yourself; it is a gift you give to yourself.

The first and most important step is to acknowledge and be aware of the harm that was done to you. The next step is that you have to be willing to feel the pain, express the anger, and then you will be ready. Forgiveness set you free and makes you feel better about yourself, and your self-love and self-respect will increase.

The next step is to forgive yourself. This step is crucial if you want to feel good about yourself.

Exercise:

1.Make a list of all the judgments about yourself and forgive yourself.

2.Stop self-criticism just for today and see what changes.

3.Write a list of 5 ways you are not loving to yourself. Be aware and then take 1 of them from the list and practice love.

4.Identify five of your most natural strengths and talents.

Example:

Make a list of all the judgments about yourself and forgive yourself.

- I am stupid.
- I am incapable.
- I talk too much.

Stop self-criticism just for today and see what changes.

Let's say you make a mistake. For example, you are washing the dishes, and you drop a plate on the floor, and it breaks. Instead of saying things to yourself like: "Oh, I am so stupid, how did I drop the plate?" Etc. Say to yourself: "Oh, I broke the plate, is ok. I will clean the pieces on the floor and finish my dishes."

Write down a list of 5 ways you are not loving to yourself.

For example: While I am at work, I do not stop and take my break to eat. The next time you go to work make sure you take your lunch with you. Go to a quiet place, relax and eat it.

Identify five of your most natural strengths and talents.

- I am detail oriented.
- I am creative.
- I can sing beautifully.
- I am organized.
- I am punctual.

Exercise 5: Building Trust

Trust in a relationship is the most important ingredient, it is the magnetic force that keeps people together. Without trust, couples are much more likely to split in times of crises or have doubts about each other's feelings.

Without trust, you haven't got anything substantial in a relationship. You must be able to trust your partner, and she/he must be able to trust you.

1.Do not keep secrets. This does not mean you have to tell everything about yourself in your relationship, nor that you feel like you have to explain your entire life, especially your past, to your partner at every turn. It does mean that when something comes up in the present that something in your past may be relevant to, you honestly talk about it. You also don't do something important or that would have a profound impact on your relationship without telling your partner about it. You cannot act as if you are all by yourself in an intimate relationship.

2.Let your needs be known. Don't expect your partner to read your mind. This especially goes for women! You have to tell them what you need from the relationship, or else they may not understand to give it to you. Some things they will be able to figure out, but many other things they won't. Don't make assumptions that they do, or should, just know.

3.Be reliable. When you say you will do something, do it. When you have a date, show up on time, and if you are running late call and say so. Make your word law. Try not to make promises you can't keep, even if you mean well by doing so.

4.Communicate. You have to have a partner with whom you can communicate. This is why looks, all by themselves, are not important: it's because they don't guarantee communication at all. If your partner asks you questions, answer them right away and with a straight, no-nonsense answer. When you have questions, just ask them. Don't make accusations, either.

5.Believe that your partner is competent with what they do. If you think that your partner is incapable, why do you want to be with him (or her)? Believe that they can handle what you tell them, who you are, and what you need from the relationship.

Katey Lyon

Conclusion

Coping with jealousy is not easy. But if you understand the causes of jealousy and the types of jealousy you can clearly start to understand yourself. Do the exercises in this book even if you think that you do not need them, be patient and do not take your jealousy as if there is something wrong with you. There is nothing wrong with you.

I hope this book helps you to take the first steps to free yourself from your jealousy patterns.

And if you enjoyed this book, please leave a review on Amazon. Thank you!!, your feedback is important.

Katey Lyon

References

1WebMed. Seeing Green: All About Jealousy. Retrieved from: http://www.webmd.com/sex-relationships/features/overcoming-jealousy

2.NetPlaces. Behind the Need to Control Your Partner. Retrieved from: http://www.netplaces.com/happy-marriage/the-self-in-marriage/behind-the-need-to-control-your-partner.htm

3.Relationship World. Jealousy - A deep-seated Fear. Retrieved from: http://relationship-world.com/jealousy-a-deep-seated-fear/

Katey Lyon

www.ingramcontent.com/pod-product-compliance
Lightning Source LLC
Chambersburg PA
CBHW060228290526
45789CB00003B/1468

* 9 7 8 1 5 3 7 5 7 3 4 0 3 *